Home Office Research Study 168

Managing courts effectively: The reasons for adjournments in magistrates' courts

by Claire Whittaker and Alan Mackie with Ruth Lewis and Nicola Ponikiewski

A Research and Statistics Directorate Report

Home Office
Research and
Statistics
Directorate

London: Home Office

Home Office Research Studies

The Home Office Research Studies are reports on research undertaken by or on behalf of the Home Office. They cover the range of subjects for which the Home Secretary has responsibility. Titles in the series are listed at the back of this report (copies are available from the address on the back cover). Other publications produced by the Research and Statistics Directorate include Research Findings, the Research Bulletin, Statistical Bulletins and Statistical Papers.

The Research and Statistics Directorate

The Directorate consists of three Units which deal with research and statistics on Crime and Criminal Justice, Offenders and Corrections, Immigration and General Matters; the Programme Development Unit; the Economics Unit; and the Operational Research Unit.

The Research and Statistics Directorate is an integral part of the Home Office, serving the Ministers and the department itself, its services, Parliament and the public through research, development and statistics. Information and knowledge from these sources informs policy development and the management of programmes; their dissemination improves wider public understanding of matters of Home Office concern.

First published 1997

Application for reproduction should be made to the Information and Publications Group, Room 1308, Home Office, Apollo House, 36 Wellesley Road, Croydon CR9 3RR.

©Crown copyright 1997 ISBN 1 85893 804 X
ISSN 0072 6435

Foreword

There has long been concern about the extent of delays in magistrates' courts throughout England and Wales. In recent years there have been a number of initiatives to reduce the number of adjournments. This paper reports the findings of a survey of adjournments in 25 magistrates' courts which established the main sources of delay. Magistrates and Justices' Clerks were interviewed in 12 of the 25 courts to find out their views on the causes of delay and to see how they tried to avoid unnecessary adjournments.

DAVID MOXON
Head of the Crime and Criminal Justice Unit
Research and Statistics Directorate

Acknowledgements

We would like to thank all the Magistrates and Justices' Clerks who gave up their time to speak to us. We are also most grateful to all the court staff who made us welcome at the 25 magistrates courts that took part in the survey.

Claire Whittaker
Alan Mackie
Ruth Lewis
Nicola Ponikiewski

Contents

Summary

There has long been concern about the extent to which cases are adjourned in magistrates' courts. This study reports the findings of a survey of the reasons for adjournments in 25 courts throughout England and Wales. The findings were supplemented by interviews with magistrates and justices' clerks in 12 of the 25 courts.

The main findings of the research were:

- The most frequent reason for an adjournment was that either the prosecution or defence were not ready to proceed prior to trial (although in many instances it was not possible for observers to discern the reasons for this lack of readiness from what was said in court). Together these accounted for just over half (54%) of adjournments.

- There were large variations between courts in the reasons for adjournments: for example, the proportion of adjournments which took place because the defence was not able to proceed accounted for between 37 and three per cent of adjournments in indictable cases. Similarly the proportion of adjournments which took place because advance disclosure had not been served varied between 12 per cent and none. This suggested that differing local practices were causing variations in the types of adjournments that occurred.

- In six per cent of cases advance disclosure of the prosecution case had not been given to the defence. Where advance disclosure was provided on the day of the hearing many magistrates put the case back until later if that would allow the defence time to look at it and the case progress that day.

- Five per cent of adjournments occurred because legal aid had not been decided. Some magistrates and justices' clerks felt that the new legal aid arrangements could lead to extra delays as defendants have to provide more documentation of their income.

- Magistrates were doubtful whether the sentence discounts for a guilty plea were sufficient incentive to defendants to plead guilty at an early stage and therefore avoid 'cracked' trials. Once the limited nature of magistrates' sentencing powers were taken into account, the discount made little tangible difference to the actual length of time served in a custodial sentence. They also doubted whether defendants appreciated the difference that the discount made to sentences other than custody.

- Seven of the 12 courts where interviews were held had introduced pre-trial reviews (PTR) in order to make sure that the case was ready to progress to trial. Most of the justices' clerks in these courts felt that the PTR was effective as a way of reducing the incidence of cracked trials by as much as 40 per cent. However one court had abandoned PTRs because it had become simply another appearance where the trial date was fixed. In some courts PTRs were reserved for trials expected to last more than a day.

- The second most frequent reason for an adjournment was because further information was required to assist sentencing – most often a pre-sentence report, but sometimes a medical or psychiatric report. This accounted for 10 per cent of adjournments. An adjournment for a report to be prepared was considered necessary in almost all cases where a custodial or community sentence was considered.

- One-fifth of adjournments in summary motoring cases were because information was needed from the DVLA on previous motoring endorsements.

- Some courts reported delays in obtaining information on the defendant's previous convictions from the police.

- Magistrates and justices' clerks in a quarter of the courts where interviews took place said that they had used the court users' group as a forum to raise issues to do with the management of court business that involved all the various groups and also to highlight particular cases where they felt there had been unacceptable delays.

- Bench Chairmen had received training to encourage them to question the need for adjournments. This encouraged a court culture in which all parties realised that there had to be a 'good reason' why a case should be adjourned. They also asked court clerks to record the reason why an adjournment was granted so that repeated adjournments were not given for the same reason.

- Courts had developed different methods of listing in order to best manage the throughput of business. Scheduling cases was described as an 'inexact science' and many 'overlisted' each courtroom in anticipation that a proportion of cases would not go ahead as planned.

- Gaps in court business in seven of the 12 courts where interviews took place were filled by a 'floating' list of road traffic cases in which the defendant had pleaded guilty by post. Most justices' clerks did not list floating trials because they felt that the prosecutor would be disadvantaged if he or she had not had a chance to prepare the case before the trial began.

1 Introduction

'Justice delayed is justice denied' is a phrase that is frequently heard in the criminal justice system and the question of the length of time taken to deal with cases has excited considerable interest over the years in both magistrates' courts and the Crown Court. However, in the mid 1980s, published statistics showed that the time taken to finish cases in magistrates' courts was increasing. This, combined with new styles of management in the public sector[1] which place considerable weight on the efficient use of resources, led to a number of initiatives aimed at reducing delays in the courts. In particular, there have been attempts to reduce the number of occasions that a case appears in court prior to completion. Despite these initiatives, an annual survey of the number of adjournments showed that the average number of times that a case is adjourned was unchanged in 1996 on 1995 at 2.6 per case. This was slightly higher than in 1994 when the average number of adjournments in indictable cases was 2.4.[2] There are significant differences between courts in their adjournment rate: in the 25 courts in this study the average number of adjournments per case for all offences ranged between 0.7 and 2.1 in 1993. For indictable offences, the average ranged from 1.8 to 3.2 per case in 1993.[3]

Although some of these differences will be explained by case mix, much of it must be due to other factors. This study examined the reasons for adjournments in magistrates' courts. It also aimed to identify good practice which could be adopted to improve efficiency in some areas.

---

1   Since the early 1980s private sector styles and techniques of management have increasingly been seen throughout the public sector in most Western countries including the UK. This managerial approach has taken the efficient use of resources as one of the indicators of success. All the main organisations in the criminal justice system - the police, CPS, probation service and the prison service as well as the courts - have undergone significant changes in management structure and organisational cultures and practices. (See Raine and Wilson (1995) for a further discussion of the impact of new public management on criminal justice organisations.)

2   Source: Time intervals for proceedings in indictable cases in magistrates' courts *Information Bulletin* 2/96 Lord Chancellor's Department.

3   For summary non-motoring offences the average number of adjournments in the 25 courts ranged between 0.1 and 1.2 while for summary motoring offences it ranged from 0.7 to 2.0 per case. It should be noted that these are taken from a sample of cases appearing in one week and for some smaller courts the averages are calculated on small numbers.

Information on adjournments was recorded in a survey of 4,577 hearings where an adjournment was requested and no other procedure took place.[4] The fieldwork took place between July 1994 and May 1995 and data was collected over a four to six week period in each of the 25 courts. Cases where a plea was entered by post were omitted, which meant that the sample excluded most summary motoring cases. Adjournments are not a significant issue in these cases, and the majority of these cases are dealt with at their first court appearance. The sample focuses on those cases where an adjournment was most likely to occur and where, because all participants are present in court, they have the most impact. The sample excluded cases which were adjourned by justices' clerks under the powers given to them by the Magistrates' Courts (Miscellaneous Amendments) Rules 1993 and so focused on adjournments agreed by magistrates. The survey was supplemented by 28 group interviews with magistrates (126 in total) and interviews with justices' clerks in 12 of the areas that had participated in the original survey.

Chapter 2 of this report discusses a number of initiatives that have been introduced to reduce delay and examines the views of magistrates and justices' clerks on these in relation to adjournments. Chapters 3 and 4 concentrate on the results of the survey of adjournment hearings. The findings are discussed in chapter 5.

---

4   This was part of a wide-ranging study covering sentencing, fine enforcement, mode of trial decisions and remands. The study was not, therefore, concerned simply with adjournments, but the fact of having observers in court provided an opportunity to record some details which would not be available from court records. However, its limitation was that it was not practicable to investigate in more depth reasons *why*, for example, the prosecution or defence were not ready to proceed where this was not made clear in court.

2 Initiatives to reduce delay

In magistrates' courts one of the key indicators of efficiency has been taken to be a low adjournment rate. The decision to grant an adjournment is a judicial decision and the Magistrates' Association have also expressed concern about the increasing numbers of adjournments. While recognising that there are many legitimate reasons for seeking an adjournment in the interests of justice, the Association issued guidance to help encourage magistrates and in particular bench chairmen to conduct inquiries to establish why an adjournment is required (Magistrates' Association, 1993). Against this background of concern and incentives to reduce delay, several initiatives have been introduced in recent years.

Delegated Clerks' Powers

The Magistrates' Courts (Miscellaneous Amendments) Rules were introduced in 1993, following recommendations of a working group of representatives of the Magistrates' Association, Justices' Clerks' Society and the CPS, in order to simplify and speed up procedures. The Rules gave increased powers to justices' clerks to undertake procedures that were previously dealt with by magistrates, one of which was the ability to grant an adjournment where both parties were in agreement. Clerks are also able to extend police bail where the CPS are in agreement, enlarge court bail (although not to vary bail conditions), carry out paper committals for bailed defendants, take pleas and set or change trial dates. It was envisaged that the powers would be used flexibly so that, for example, adjournments could be made by letter, fax or telephone.

A survey of the extent to which justices' clerks used these powers was carried out in 1994 (Home Office, 1994). It found that almost all (96 %) of justices' clerks used some or all of them and only one in ten said that they never used their delegated powers to make adjournments. The survey found that the powers were most useful where a special court had been established to deal with business using the delegated powers.[1] Reasons why

---

1   These are often referred to as 'clerks' courts'.

courts had not established dedicated courts included the non-availability of prosecutors or defence lawyers and a lack of space. Some clerks felt that the magistrates in their area could cope with the workload in court and so there was no need to set up other procedures to divert work away from the bench.

Scheduling

Various steps have been taken to improve the scheduling of cases in the court list and in 1991 the Home Office produced a good practice guide to help courts improve their scheduling (Home Office, 1991). Almost all magistrates' courts now have a 'listing officer' who has responsibility for organising the dates and timing of hearings. In some areas the listing officer will check whether the case is ready to proceed to trial by contacting all parties concerned: in one study this was found to happen in one of the seven clerkships that were looked at, but frequently one or more of the parties involved did not provide information on the progress of the case (Raine and Wilson, 1992).

'Block listing' is another initiative to improve the daily scheduling used by many courts in this study. However the term 'block listing' includes a wide range of arrangements: in interviews, eight of the 12 Clerks said that they used block listing but further questioning revealed that some used an appointments system with each case being allocated a specific time slot whilst others simply listed certain types of case on specific days. An example of the most elaborate form of block listing was a court which listed criminal cases for 10.00, 10.30 and 11.00 am while the Family Court ran an appointment system.[2] However, in another court it had been found that it was not possible to use block listing in the means enquiry court because a large proportion of defendants did not attend in court. Four of the eight courts where listing was studied in more detail used a more limited form of block listing: a typical example of how work is allocated was given by one clerk who explained that in the morning remand and custody cases are allocated to one court room and bail, guilty pleas, sentences and reports are heard in a second court room. The other three benches will deal with trials, and in the afternoon, courts are listed with specific types of cases, such as road traffic etc.

Three of the 12 courts used a much less elaborate form of block listing in which cases were scheduled to appear either in the morning or afternoon. A clerk at one of these courts explained that he had reviewed a neighbouring

---

2   In that court the 'appointment' system was thought to work well in the family court, but precise morning lists had been abandoned in the criminal court because defence solicitors found it difficult to get to the right court at the correct time when they were dealing with a number of cases appearing in different court rooms (Court 10).

court's experience of block listing and found that delays were caused by defendants, and sometimes solicitors, not attending appointments.

Justices' clerks recognised that it is impossible for scheduling to be precise. Clerks in seven of the 12 courts used a floating list of road traffic cases in which the defendant had pleaded guilty by letter and so could be dealt with quickly to fill gaps in court business. In the Crown Court it is common for a number of trials to be listed for a day but, rather than being allocated to a particular court room, they are slotted into court rooms that become vacant as other cases finish. Almost all the justices' clerks (11 of 12) that were interviewed did not feel that this would be appropriate in magistrates' courts. In the Crown Court the prosecution and defence barristers are present solely to appear in one case and so can easily move to a different court room. The situation is different in magistrates' courts where one prosecutor will deal with all the cases which appear in one courtroom. If the prosecutor was asked to take on a 'floating trial', it is likely that he or she would be unfamiliar with the case and so be disadvantaged in the proceedings.

Pre-trial Reviews

This research found a widespread concern about the number of cracked trials (i.e. cases where the defendant changed his or her plea to guilty on the day that the trial was due to start). Many justices' clerks (seven out of ten interviewed) had introduced pre-trial reviews (PTRs) to tackle this problem. Although PTRs were widely used, some of the clerks were uncertain whether the procedure effectively reduced the numbers of cracked trials. For example, one magistrate from a court which used PTR in cases which were likely to last for more than one day, said that:

> *they are largely ineffective and [have become] simply another date at which we fix a date for trial. (Magistrate, Court 9)*

Other clerks had found the procedure to be more successful in preventing cracked trials: e.g. one clerk claimed that the introduction of PTR had reduced the number of cracked trials by over 40 per cent. Many clerks reported that they 'overlisted' trials in anticipation that a proportion of them would not go ahead.[3]

---

3   The problem with this approach was that, if most of the trials that were listed did go ahead, a proportion would have to put off to another day which inconvenienced all parties concerned with them.

Discount for a guilty plea

It is well established sentencing practice that offenders who plead guilty may be given a lighter sentence than those who fight the case to the bitter end and are convicted. The discount can be expected to be within the range of 25 - 33 per cent of the sentence that would have been given if they had pleaded not guilty (Morton, 1994:27-9). The Criminal Justice and Public Order Act 1994 (s 48) formalised this established practice. Although the Act did not introduce a formal procedure of sentence discounts, it stated that, in considering whether to give a lighter sentence than would be expected if the defendant pleaded not guilty, the Court should take into account (i) the stage at which the intention to plead guilty was announced and (ii) the circumstances in which the intention to plead guilty was given. It was expected that the introduction of the discount would reduce the number of cracked trials by giving the defendant an incentive to plead guilty at an early opportunity.

While many magistrates said that they made a point of announcing the fact that they had given a lighter sentence because the defendant had pleaded guilty, they expressed doubts that the discount provided sufficient incentive to plead guilty. The maximum sentence which can be imposed in the magistrates' courts in most circumstances is six months which may be reduced to four months if the offender pleads guilty. Once the automatic early release arrangements for offenders serving short sentences are taken into account,[4] the practical maximum effect of a sentence discount is to reduce the time spent in prison by one month (half of the maximum discount of two months). Many magistrates said that this discount was not sufficient to encourage offenders to plead guilty but recognised that it would have greater impact in the Crown Court where the sentences were much longer and the benefit to offenders in pleading guilty was more tangible. For example, magistrates in one area said that the discount for a guilty plea was:

> *more real in the Crown Court... than in the magistrates' court where it applies to a lesser extent (Magistrate, Court 6, Group 3).*

They also said that the sentence discount provided less incentive where the defendant was likely to receive a non-custodial sentence:

---

4   Following the Criminal Justice Act 1991, offenders serving less than four years are automatically released after serving half of their sentence subject to any additional days imposed for offences committed while in prison.

I don't think that [offenders] can judge the difference that a discount makes: an 18 month probation order becomes a year, well that doesn't mean anything to them. The only way it means anything is on the length of custody or possibly community service. (Magistrate, Court 1, Group 3)

Court users groups

Courts have been encouraged to foster inter-agency co-operation by establishing 'court user groups' to provide a forum for discussion about a range of topics including the scheduling which affects all the main professional users of the court – the police, Crown Prosecution Service (CPS), probation service and regular duty solicitors. Clerks and magistrates in four of the 12 courts said that they used the court users group to discuss adjournments: some had used the group as a way of conveying the message that the magistrates would be taking a tougher line on adjournments, whilst others had referred cases in which magistrates thought there had been unacceptable delays to illustrate particular problems.

Time targets for stages in criminal process

The appropriate time intervals for the different stages of criminal procedures were considered by the inter-departmental Working Group on Pre-Trial Issues which recommended a set of targets for the length of time it should take to complete various tasks and stages in the preparation and conduct of a case through the pre-trial process. For example the Working Group recommended that a national guideline of two weeks should be adopted to enable the police to provide an abbreviated file of evidence to the CPS. When the CPS receives notification from the court naming the defence solicitor, advance disclosure should be sent automatically to the solicitor by the CPS. They also recommended that advance disclosure should be prepared automatically and made available at the first court hearing in circumstances where there has been no notification from the court of the defence solicitor's details and no request from the defence for disclosure. In order for the time targets to be met, very close liaison is required between all the criminal justice agencies.

Obstacles to improvement

The task of improving scheduling in courts remains formidable. Court business is dependent on the presence of a number of people – the magistrates, the clerk and support staff, a prosecutor, defence solicitor, defendant(s), a probation officer and, if a trial takes place, witnesses for the prosecution and defence – and it can be difficult for the court to ensure that all of these people appear simultaneously. This problem is compounded because there is no one main customer or 'lead' agency who can set the timetable to which the others must conform. This is in contrast to other service settings where most interactions are one-to-one (for example, between doctor and patient) or where there is often an acknowledged hierarchy of agencies or professionals where one will take a lead in setting the timetable. In most other public services, the recipients are usually motivated to co-operate because they are seeking a beneficial outcome. To take a simple example, a patient will usually seek an appointment with a doctor because they are concerned about their symptoms. In contrast, some of the parties in the criminal justice system have no incentive to facilitate the progress of the case. Rather, some defendants may be keen to delay the progress of the case in order to put off the day of reckoning (Raine and Wilson, 1992:3).

The Magistrates' Association (1993) has produced guidance for Bench Chairmen to encourage them to question the reasons why an adjournment is necessary. In interviews, many magistrates said that they were beginning to take the lead and be more inquisitorial in questioning why a solicitor was seeking an adjournment. For example, one magistrate said:

> *I think that we are very well trained and that there are very few chair people who are not constantly asking questions. Every time there is a request for a delay it is questioned ... I don't know if we are speeding anything up, but at least it embarrasses people. (Magistrate, Court 10, Group 2)*

Many justices' clerks explained that in their training Bench Chairmen were encouraged to scrutinise applications for adjournments rather than grant them unquestioningly. One clerk said that magistrates were trained to:

> *....take a structured approach to applications for adjournments, to question all cases and their reasons for adjournments... [however] magistrates are still reluctant to refuse an adjournment where the prosecution and the defence put forward a joint application. I think that there is a need to go further in enquiring into the reasons for adjournments. (Justices' Clerk, Court 12)*

Some magistrates had adopted the practice of asking the clerk to note the reason that was given for adjournment so that they could monitor the progress of the case and avoid repeated adjournments:

> *[I] make sure if they do grant an adjournment they actually*

announce the expectation for the next hearing. We are also keen that the [court] clerks give a history of the case to the magistrates prior to them considering an adjournment. (Magistrate, Court 12)

This inquisition is, however, conducted against the need to ensure that justice is seen to be done. As one clerk explained that:

I start from the premise that the case should proceed, unless there is a good reason to the contrary. Illness is a good example of that. On the other hand, if it is something that is in [the party's control] then it seems to me that there comes a time to say ... it is not in the interests of justice to adjourn further. (Justices' Clerk, Court 11)

However justices' clerks also have a role to play. One clerk admitted that, when faced with a long list of cases, it was tempting for a clerk to adjourn matters in order to get through the day's work. He explained that:

....it doesn't help the administration of justice in the long run. I have spent some time with the court clerks saying that if your bench are not proactive, then you have to be proactive. You've got to be searching and you've got to justify an adjournment. (Justices Clerk, Court 9)

Legal constraints

Perhaps the most important difference between the pursuit of efficiency in criminal justice compared to other areas of social policy is that, because the state exercises considerable coercive power through the criminal justice system, there are a number of legal constraints which have to be observed in managing the system: a simple example of this is where a person pleads not guilty a trial must be arranged. In situations where the protection of an accused person's rights may be in conflict with the most efficient management of court resources, the former must take precedence. Also, criminal cases have to follow a legally defined process, departure from which can cause the case to fail. This means that the capacity of a manager to reduce procedures is strictly limited by statute, and magistrates' scope for insisting that a case proceeds is restricted.

3 The reasons for adjournments

This section reports the findings of a survey of cases where an adjournment was given in court. Table 3.1 shows the reasons that were given.

Table 3.1 The reasons given for adjournments[1]

Reasons stated in court	n	percentage of cases in which factor was mentioned
Pre-trial – Case not ready to proceed	**2,472**	**54.0**
Defence were not able to proceed	944	20.6
CPS were not able to proceed	905	19.8
Defence requesting advance disclosure which has not been provided yet	260	5.7
Defence applying for legal aid /legal aid not yet decided	226	4.9
Solicitor not available in court /seeking other legal advice	98	2.1
For consultation between the CPS and defence	27	0.6
Further police enquiries are necessary	12	0.2
Further information required	**730**	**16.9**
Pre-sentence report requested	384	8.4
Further information needed e.g. recent previous convictions	147	3.2
Medical or psychiatric report requested	92	2.0
Information needed from DVLA on previous driving convictions	85	1.9
Information required from the victim for compensation	16	0.3
Newton hearing to take place	6	0.1

continued

Table 3.1 The reasons given for adjournments (continued)

	n	percentage of cases in which factor was mentioned
Adjourned to a trial date	642	**14.0**
Entered a not guilty plea and a trial date is set	580	12.7
To a pre-trial review	62	1.4
Case awaiting committal to the Crown Court	488	**10.7**
Defendant not present	642	**14.0**
Defendant failed to appear at court	485	10.6
Defendant not produced at court from prison	84	1.8
Defendant not present because of illness	73	1.6
Remitted to another court	287	**6.3**
To be heard on same day as other charges which are before the Court	144	3.1
To be heard with other codefendants in the same case	91	2.0
To be heard in the youth court	39	0.9
Case remitted to another court e.g. because the person has other cases being heard there	13	0.3
Other	215	**4.7**
Other reason	155	3.4
Interpreter required	20	0.4
Court business overran the available time	12	0.3
Police to administer a caution	17	0.4
Awaiting the outcome of other charges before sentencing	11	0.2
Total number of reasons stated	**5,476**	

*NOTE*1. A number of reasons could be stated to explain why an adjournment was necessary. The average number of reasons given per case was 1.2.

---

1   It is possible that this figure included some cases in which the defendant appeared from police custody having been arrested the previous day. The CPS would not have been able to provide advance disclosure in this situation. It is a limitation of the study that the proportion of defendants appearing from police custody was not known.

Case not ready to proceed

The most frequently stated reason for a case to be adjourned was because it was not ready to proceed prior to trial i.e. the CPS and/or the defence were not ready to proceed (Table 3.1). In the majority of cases it was not known exactly why the case was not ready to go ahead but in six per cent the defence had not been served with advance disclosure of the prosecution case prior to the hearing.1 However, in three of the 12 courts where interviews were held, magistrates and clerks said that the situation was improving and in some instances disclosure was available on the day of the hearing:

> *The CPS are much quicker at getting papers ready for disclosure... the defendant's solicitor may, however, want more information. (Magistrate, Court 6, Group 3)*

In straightforward cases where advance disclosure is available on the day, the Magistrates' Association has urged the bench to consider putting the case back until later in the day to allow the defence to read the advance disclosure and take instructions from the defendant. One magistrate explained that:

> *it is not always necessary to grant an adjournment if you have the courage of your convictions and ask the parties if they could deal with the matter over lunch. (Magistrate, Court 11, Group 1)*

In five per cent of cases legal aid had not been decided. Magistrates and clerks in two of the 12 courts felt that the legal aid scheme itself acted as a disincentive for defence solicitors to expedite matters. They believed that there was no incentive for solicitors to ensure that their clients attended court; if the client did not turn up, the matter was adjourned and the solicitor earned more fee income. In other courts, magistrates believed that the new legal aid fee structure would change this as solicitors would earn a fixed fee for the work that they did, irrespective of the number of times they attended court. However, three of the 12 justices' clerks said that the new legal aid arrangements caused additional delays because clients were now required to provide documentation of their income which took some time. One of these clerks explained that:

> *We are trying to overcome this particular problem by educating solicitors to get their information ready as early as possible. (Justices' Clerk, Court 12)*

In a further two per cent of cases in the sample, an adjournment was needed because the defendant was either seeking legal advice or his or her solicitor was not available. Many magistrates complained that cases had to be adjourned because defence solicitors needed further time to take instructions from their client. Even where a case is not adjourned to another date, the timetable can be disturbed if a case has to be put back to allow solicitors to take instructions. As one magistrate explained:

> *Solicitors will not see their clients until the morning of their appearance and we are asked to give them 10 minutes to see their client ... it's a kind of justice thing, if one doesn't see the person who's meant to be representing them until just before court, it doesn't exactly inspire confidence... I would hate it, how can they do their best under such circumstances? (Magistrate, Court 8, Group 2)*

However magistrates appreciated that it was often difficult for defence solicitors to obtain instructions because many defendants lead 'chaotic and disorganised' lives and often wait until the last minute before seeking legal advice:

> *[Defendants] will leave it until the day they appear in court and will say, 'Oh, there's my solicitor!', and an adjournment will be granted. (Magistrate, Court 1)*

Magistrates felt that adjournments in these circumstances were often necessary in the 'interests of justice'. This was expressed by one magistrate who said:

> *Some people have terribly chaotic lives and there are all sorts of circumstances that you have to take into account in the interests of justice. (Magistrate, Court 4, Group 2)*

However, one clerk believed that it was necessary to take a firm stand with requests for adjournments where the defendant had not instructed a solicitor by the time of the hearing:

> *My approach to that is, the defendant had three months to instruct a solicitor, and that is the client's problem. That is not a good reason for adjourning. (Justices' Clerk, Court 11)*

In a small number of cases (12), it was not possible to proceed because further police enquiries were necessary. In such cases an adjournment is inevitable although, with the prosecution's agreement, it could be dealt with by the justices' clerk outside of the court._Magistrates in seven of the 12 areas were concerned that there seemed be a lack of co-operation between the police and the CPS which resulted in delays. For example, one magistrate said:

the major fault lies in the relationship between the CPS and the police. There is not a good enough relationship between them. (Magistrate, Court 2)

Other sources of delay which were mentioned by magistrates and clerks during the interviews were the difficulty in obtaining forensic evidence, not informing witnesses of the date they were expected at court, and problems in serving summons papers.

Further information was required

The second most frequently given reason for adjournments (17% of cases) was because the court required further information, usually before sentencing. Over half of the cases adjourned for further information (8% of the total number of adjournments) were for a pre-sentence report (PSR) to be prepared by the probation service. Although recent legislation has removed the legal requirement to have a pre-sentence report before sentencing an offender to custody,[2] a recent study found that a PSR was prepared in over four-fifths (84%) of cases which received a custodial sentence. The most common reason for dispensing with a PSR was either where a report had been prepared for another recent court appearance or where the time spent remanded in custody waiting for a report to be prepared would be the equivalent of a short sentence (Charles et al., 1997). A typical scenario where a magistrate might choose to dispense with a PSR was where:

a youth who had already served 11 months [of a custodial sentence] and was back out for one month on licence and committed further burglaries. We looked at his previous PSR and used that, and sent him down for a further 12 months. (Magistrate, Court 7, Group 1)

Similarly, where magistrates are considering a custodial sentence for an offender who is, or is thought to be, mentally disordered, they are required to order a medical report if they consider it relevant. This reason was given in two per cent of adjournments in the sample.

There were some cases which had to be adjourned because the relevant information was simply not available. For example, the court will normally require a print-out from the DVLA detailing the offender's previous endorsements on their driving licence in motoring cases. The lack of

---

2   The Criminal Justice Act 1991 (amended) stated that a PSR was mandatory in all cases where a custodial or community sentence was made (except where the offence was triable only on indictment). The 1994 Criminal Justice and Public Order Act relaxed the requirement so that a PSR is no longer a legal requirement when sentencing an offender to custody or to certain community penalties for any offence.

information from the DVLA accounted for 20 per cent of adjournments in cases involving summary traffic offences. (Overall this accounted for two per cent of the adjournments.)

In three per cent of cases there was no up-to-date schedule of previous convictions available at the point of sentence or else the defendant had not produced relevant documents. Defendants often forgot to bring their driving licence, MOT or insurance details to court and so the case could not proceed. At one court the Justices' Clerk described a particular problem in obtaining previous convictions which caused delays in sentencing:

> we have huge problems with regard to the lack of previous convictions, or the state of them if we get them. We think that we are doing well if we get any record of convictions at all ... It's no good. (Justices' Clerk, Court 9)

In cases where a defendant is required to produce insurance, MOT certificates or a driving licence, the onus is on the defendant to provide these documents. Adjournments were often inevitable where the defendant did not know what documents were required or that the court would not accept a photocopy of the documents. However, one magistrate believed that not bringing the correct documentation to court was one way in which some defendants 'played the system' to postpone sentencing:

> If you know the ropes, you can make a motoring case last nine months. You don't bring your driving licence to court or ... answer the warrant when the police come round to your house. (Magistrate, Court 4, Group 1)

If the information was obtained before the defendant's first court appearance, the nature of these charges would mean that more matters could be disposed of at the first hearing. Adjournments for these reasons could be reduced by very simple measures such as clearly stating what information will be required by the court and when to produce it on the summons which the defendant receives.

The defendant was not present

There has been considerable concern at the numbers of adjournments which occur because the defendant does not appear at court. In total, these accounted for 14 per cent of adjournments. In four out of five cases where no reason was given for the defendant's absence, an arrest warrant was issued. In a small proportion of cases (2%) the defendant was not produced from prison. This can occur for a number of reasons, e.g. because a production warrant was not issued or because, if the defendant was remanded in custody on other charges or by another court, the whereabouts of the defendant may not be known until the day of the hearing. Operational reasons may also mean that the prison service is unable to produce the defendant. The non-production of the defendant from prison as a reason for granting an adjournment was cited by only one magistrate, who added that it took three weeks for the Home Office to grant a production order.

In nearly two per cent of cases the defendant was not able to be at court because they were ill. This was raised as a particular problem in one area where the possibility of people forging medical certificates or obtaining them under false pretences was raised by the magistrates and clerk. Although the fact that the defendant was ill was not a major reason for adjournments overall, there was significant local variation in the proportion of cases where the case was adjourned because the person was too ill to attend court. Two courts had a much higher proportion of cases where this was given as a reason for an adjournment: in both, the fact that the defendant was too ill to attend court was the reason for adjournment in five per cent of cases, more than three times as many as in the sample overall.

Case remitted to another court

Six per cent of adjournments were so that the case could be remitted to another court. Most of these were cases which were adjourned so that they could be heard with other charges that the defendant was facing or with co-defendants in the same case. A particular source of delay mentioned by magistrates in two of the 12 courts where interviews took place was where the defendant committed further offences following the initial charge and was not sent to trial on all the charges until the pre-trial stages of each new charge had been completed.[3] One magistrate said:

> We are now beginning to say, 'Look, it doesn't really matter how many more offences there are, the sentence cannot be any more than this' in order to speed cases along, (Magistrate, Court 12, Group 2)

A very small number of cases were remitted to the youth court (1% of the sample). This occurred when youths appeared in the adult court, for example because they were appearing from custody and no youth court was sitting that day, or because they were co-defendants with adults. There are some legal constraints in dealing with co-defendants and juvenile offenders,

---

3   The Justices' Clerks' Society and the Magistrates' Association have recently issued a joint statement aimed at reducing the number of occasions on which the hearing of some charges against an alleged offender is deferred until it is possible to proceed on later charges so to take all outstanding together. This should have the effect of reducing the number of adjournments for this reason.

which may affect the magistrates' discretion to adjourn in these cases: for example, separate trials can be conducted for co-defendants if there are good reasons to do so but upon conviction the court should sentence them with reference to other co-defendants.

Adjourned to a trial date or to committal

These adjournments (25% of cases) were inevitable in that if a not guilty plea is entered, a trial must be arranged and similarly, if a case is destined to go to the Crown Court a committal hearing must take place. However the length of time taken for the prosecution and defence to prepare the case for committal to the Crown Court or summary trial can vary and be a source of delay.

4 Reasons for adjournments: a comparison between courts

This research revealed the range of reasons that are stated in courts for adjournments. Ideally we would want to identify any key areas where improvements might be made to reduce both the length of time that criminal cases take to complete and the cost of unnecessary adjournments to the criminal justice system.

Previously the significant differences between courts in their rates of adjournments were discussed. This research examined whether the reasons stated for adjournments varied between courts. Indictable and summary cases were considered separately because they are affected by different procedures. There were two limitations to this analysis. Firstly, the way in which the data were collected meant that it was not possible to probe into the reasons that were given in court. It was not possible to find out, for example, why the prosecution or defence was not ready to proceed. Secondly, the number of adjournments observed in some of the courts was quite small. This means that the analysis must be interpreted cautiously. Nevertheless, it does reveal some interesting differences between courts in reasons for adjournments.

Table 4.1 Reasons given for adjournments in summary and indictable offences[1]

Reason	Summary Offences				Indictable Offences			
	Court with highest incidence		Court with lowest incidence		Court with highest incidence		Court with lowest incidence	
	n	%	n	%	n	%	n	%
Pre-trial – Case not ready to proceed								
Defence were not able to proceed	14/38	37	4/116	3	32/73	38	3/207	1
CPS were not able to proceed	8/38	21	2/81	3	59/143	41	13/144	9
Defence requesting advance disclosure which has not been provided	5/67	8	0	0	28/73	38	3/160	2
Defence applying for legal aid / legal aid not yet decided	5/41	12	0	0	20/104	19	0/60	0
Solicitor not available in court/ seeking other legal advice	5/43	12	0	0	9/131	7	0/85	0
Witnesses not available	3/103	3	0	0	4/131	3	0/230	0
Further information required								
Pre-sentence report requested	17/48	35	2/41	5	10/60	17	3/160	2
Further information requested e.g. on previous convictions	23/116	20	0	0	5/134	4	0/230	0
Medical or psychiatric report requested	2/43	5	0	0	3/49	6	2/230	1
Information needed from DVLA on previous driving convictions	16/146	11	0	0	-	-	-	-
Case awaiting committal to the Crown Court								
A date set for committal to Crown Court	*	*	*	*	77/184	42	2/60	3

Table 4.1 Reasons given for adjournments in summary and indictable offences

Continued

Adjourned to a trial date

Entered a not guilty plea, a trial date set	17/42	41	9/116	8	28/160	18	3/270	1
To a pre-trial review²	8/85	10	0	0	2/32	7	0/388	0

Defendant not present

Defendant failed to appear at court	38/103	37	4/71	5	35/144	24	1/143	0.6
Defendant not produced from prison	2/48	4	0/160	0	14/184	8	0/160	0
Defendant not present because of illness	5/85	6	0	0	4/82	5	0/160	0

Other

To be heard on same day as other charges which are before the Court	9/85	11	1/86	1	5/49	10	3/160	2
Interpreter required	5/123	4	0	0	4/120	3	0/160	0
To be heard with co-defendants on another day	–	–	–	–	15/85	17	0/138	0

Total number of summary cases	1,714
Total number indictable cases	2,803

Notes

1. Some of the reasons mentioned in Table 3.1 were omitted from this analysis because of the small number of cases in which they were cited.

2. *** Not applicable in summary cases

3. Only eight of the 25 courts in the sample routinely held pre-trial reviews.

For both indictable and summary offences, Table 4.1 shows that there were significant differences in reason for adjournments stated in courts: the fact that the defence was not able to proceed was the most cited reason overall but the proportion of cases in which this reason was mentioned in court varied between 37 and three per cent in summary cases and 38 and one per cent in indictable cases. Similarly, the fact that the CPS were not able to proceed was cited in between 21 and three per cent of summary cases and 41 and nine per cent in indictable cases. It is very unlikely that these differences occurred by chance[1] and would suggest that differing local practices were resulting in variations in the numbers of adjournments for these reasons. Other areas where there were significant variations between courts in the proportions of adjournments given for specific reasons were because legal aid had not been decided yet (ranging between 12 and 0 % of cases in summary offences and 19 and 0 % in indictable offences), because the solicitor was not available or the defendant had not yet sought legal advice (ranging between 12 and 0 %, in summary cases and 7 and 0 % in indictable offences). The fact that the defence had requested advance disclosure which had not been served was a factor in between 38 and two per cent of adjournments in indictable offences and in between eight and 0 per cent of cases in summary offences.

However there were also significant differences between the courts in the proportion of adjournments that were 'unavoidable'. Table 4.2 shows that the courts with the lowest average number of adjournments had a greater proportion of adjournments for reasons that were probably unavoidable: for example 25 per cent of adjournments in courts with a lower rate of adjournments were because the case was proceeding to trial compared to 19 per cent of adjournments in courts with a higher rate of adjournments. On the other hand, the courts with higher rates of adjournments had more cases which did not proceed because either the defence and/or the prosecution was not ready. This reason accounted for 45 per cent of adjournments in courts with higher rates of adjournments compared to 37 per cent of adjournments in the courts with lower rates of adjournments. Although we do not know why the various parties were not in a position to make progress with the case when they appeared in court, this analysis supports the hypothesis that this is the area of court business where improvements can be made to further 'chip away' at the number of adjournments. Further research would be needed to look in detail at the reasons why the CPS and defence are not always ready to proceed with cases.

---

1   Both findings were statistically significant at the 5 per cent level.

Table 4.2 Reasons for adjournments by average rate of adjournments in the courts[1]

Main reason stated in court	8 Courts with a below average number of adjournments per case	17 Courts with an average/ higher than average number of adjournments per case
	%	%
Defence and/or prosecution not ready	37	45
Defendant did not attend Court	14	12
Trial or committal date set	25	19
Reports or further information required	14	13
Remitted to another court	4	6
Other	6	4
Total number of cases	1,493	3,081

Note:

1. Courts were classified on the basis of annually collected statistics on the average number of adjournments in indictable cases. Information was missing on three cases.

5 Discussion

This research has demonstrated the range of reasons that are given in courts for adjournments and, importantly, it has revealed areas where measures could be taken to reduce the number of adjournments and so reduce the length of time that criminal cases take to reach completion and also save the cost of repeated adjournments. For example, the study highlighted the fact that 20 per cent of adjournments in summary motoring cases are because information was not available from the DVLA. Experimental schemes are currently being run by the Home Office which provide courts with a direct computer link to the DVLA and should mean that the number of adjournments occurring for this reason can be substantially reduced. Another approach which aims to reduce adjournments in minor motoring cases involves proving cases at their first appearance rather than adjourning the case to allow the defendant another chance to reply to the summons.[1] At the court where this operated, 80 per cent of such cases were disposed of at the first occasion.

Other adjournments which might be avoided by better pre-court preparation by one or more parties involved are those where the case is not able to proceed because advance disclosure is not available, legal aid has not been decided or because the person was not produced from prison. Significant differences were observed between the courts in the reasons that were stated for adjournments. The greatest variations were in the proportion of cases that were adjourned pre-trial because the case was not ready to proceed. In particular, there was a great deal of variation in the proportions of adjournments that took place because the defence was not able to proceed and in the proportion of cases which were adjourned because the CPS was not able to proceed. These variations were very unlikely to have occurred by chance and it was suggested that differing local practices could result in variations in the reasons why adjournments took place. All these findings together suggest that the area where improvements could be made to reduce the number of adjournments was in the area of the preparation of cases prior to trial.

---

1   In most motoring cases, if the defendant does not reply to the court summons, and there is evidence that the defendant received the summons, the case will be adjourned to allow the defendant more time to respond.

This conclusion is supported by previous work on managing court business which has pointed to the importance of organisational culture in influencing procedures and working practices in courts.[2] In their study of scheduling in magistrates' courts, Raine and Wilson (1992) compared eight clerkships with widely differing delay rate and examined organisational cultures to examine the factors which contributed to efficiency in courts. The factor which was identified as the most influential was the extent to which the court was prepared to take the lead in organising court business. In particular they argued that the significant differences could be explained by the extent to which clerkships believed that they could take responsibility for controlling business to make court users accountable to the court and to negotiate with the various agencies to establish effective relationships with the main professional users. They concluded that:

> *Culture ... is likely to be the key determinant of performance with regard to delay, convenience to parties and use of court resources... courts have a choice to make over the kind of culture which they wish to project. (Raine and Wilson 1992:60)*

Magistrates and justices' clerks felt that sentencers were now much more active in questioning the need for adjournments than they had been previously. Bench chairmen had received training to encourage them to explore the reasons why an adjournment was being requested rather than simply granting a request automatically.

However magistrates and justices' clerks recognised that the decision to grant adjournments involves balancing the smooth running of the court with the interests of justice so that neither the prosecution nor the defendant are disadvantaged. There will always be some need for adjournments but it is necessary to 'chip away' at the reasons for adjournments taking place to reduce them as much as possible while recognising that there will always be some cases that do not go ahead as planned. This report has highlighted ways in which some courts attempted to reduce the number of adjournments and shown some of the problems which are associated with these initiatives. It has also suggested that the main area where adjournments could be reduced is the number of cases which do not proceed because the prosecution and/or the defence are not ready to proceed. Further research might usefully examine the reasons why cases did not proceed in detail and compare working practices between courts with high and low rates of adjournments.

---

2   See for example Church *et al.* (1978).

References

Charles, N., Whittaker, C., and Ball C., (1997) *Sentencing without a pre-sentence report.* Home Office Research Findings No 47.

Church, T. W., Carlson, A., Lee, J. and Tan, T., (1978) *Justice delayed: the pace of litigation in urban trial courts.* National Centre for State Courts.

Home Office, (1991) *Listing, Report of the Best Practice Advisory Group.* London: HMSO.

Home Office, (1994) *Magistrates' Courts (Miscellaneous Amendments) Rules 1993 Survey.* Unpublished.

Lord Chancellor's Department, (1996) *Time Intervals for proceedings in indictable cases in magistrates' courts:* February 1996 Information Bulletin 2/96.

Magistrates' Association, (1993) *'The Avoidance of delays in the Magistrates' Court'.* Magistrate 49 pp. 69-73.

Morton, J., (1994) *A guide to the Criminal Justice and Public Order Act 1994* London: Butterworths.

Raine, J.W., and Wilson, M.J., (1992) *The CDE of Scheduling in Magistrates' Courts. RPU* Occasional Papers. London :Home Office.

Raine, J.W., and Wilson, M.J., (1995) 'New Public Management and Criminal Justice'. *Public Money and Management* January-March pp. 35-40 CIPFA.

Publications

List of research publications

A list of research reports for the last three years is provided below. A **full** list of publications is available on request from the Research and Statistics Directorate Information and Publications Group.

Home Office Research Studies (HORS)

133. **Intensive Probation in England and Wales: an evaluation.** George Mair, Charles Lloyd, Claire Nee and Rae Sibbett. 1994. xiv + 143pp. (0 11 341114 6).

134. **Contacts between Police and Public: findings from the 1992 British Crime Survey.** Wesley G Skogan. 1995. ix + 93pp. (0 11 341115 4).

135. **Policing low-level disorder: Police use of Section 5 of the Public Order Act 1986.** David Brown and Tom Ellis. 1994. ix + 69pp. (0 11 341116 2).

136. **Explaining reconviction rates: A critical analysis.** Charles Lloyd, George Mair and Mike Hough. 1995. xiv + 103pp. (0 11 341117 0).

137. **Case Screening by the Crown Prosecution Service: How and why cases are terminated.** Debbie Crisp and David Moxon. 1995. viii + 66pp. (0 11 341137 5).

138. **Public Interest Case Assessment Schemes.** Debbie Crisp, Claire Whittaker and Jessica Harris. 1995. x + 58pp. (0 11 341139 1).

139. **Policing domestic violence in the 1990s.** Sharon Grace. 1995. x + 74pp. (0 11 341140 5).

140. **Young people, victimisation and the police: British Crime Survey findings on experiences and attitudes of 12 to 15 year olds.** Natalie Aye Maung. 1995. xii + 140pp. (0 11 341150 2).

141. **The Settlement of refugees in Britain.** Jenny Carey-Wood, Karen Duke, Valerie Karn and Tony Marshall. 1995. xii + 133pp. (0 11 341145 6).

142. **Vietnamese Refugees since 1982.** Karen Duke and Tony Marshall. 1995. x + 62pp. (0 11 341147 2).

143. **The Parish Special Constables Scheme.** Peter Southgate, Tom Bucke and Carole Byron. 1995. x + 59pp. (1 85893 458 3).

144. **Measuring the Satisfaction of the Courts with the Probation Service.** Chris May. 1995. x + 76pp. (1 85893 483 4).

145. **Young people and crime.** John Graham and Benjamin Bowling. 1995. xv + 142pp. (1 85893 551 2).

146. **Crime against retail and manufacturing premises: findings from the 1994 Commercial Victimisation Survey.** Catriona Mirrlees-Black and Alec Ross. 1995. xi + 110pp. (1 85893 554 7).

147. **Anxiety about crime: findings from the 1994 British Crime Survey.** Michael Hough. 1995. viii + 92pp. (1 85893 553 9).

148. **The ILPS Methadone Prescribing Project.** Rae Sibbitt. 1996. viii + 69pp. (1 85893 485 0).

149. **To scare straight or educate? The British experience of day visits to prison for young people.** Charles Lloyd. 1996. xi + 60pp. (1 85893 570 9).

150. **Predicting reoffending for Discretionary Conditional Release.** John B Copas, Peter Marshall and Roger Tarling. 1996. vii + 49pp. (1 85893 576 8).

151. **Drug misuse declared: results of the 1994 British Crime Survey.** Malcolm Ramsay and Andrew Percy. 1996. xv + 131pp. (1 85893 628 4).

152. **An Evaluation of the Introduction and Operation of the Youth Court.** David O'Mahony and Kevin Haines. 1996. viii + 70pp. (1 85893 579 2).

153. **Fitting supervision to offenders: assessment and allocation decisions in the Probation Service.** Ros Burnett. 1996. xi + 99pp. (1 85893 599 7).

154. **Ethnic minorities: victimisation and racial harassment. Findings fro the 1988 and 1992 British Crime Surveys.** Marian FitzGerald and Chris Hale. 1996. xi + 97pp. (1 85893 6039).

155. **PACE ten years on: a review of the research.** David Brown. 1996. xx + 280pp. (1 85893 603 9).

156. **Automatic Conditional Release: the first two years.** Mike Maguire, Brigitte Perroud and Peter Raynor. 1996. x + 114pp. (1 85893 659 4).

157. **Testing obscenity: an international comparison of laws and controls relating to obscene material.** Sharon Grace. 1996. ix + 46pp. (1 85893 672 1).

158. **Enforcing community sentences.** Tom Ellis, Carol Hedderman and Ed Mortimer. 1996. x + 81pp. (1 85893 691 8).

160. **Implementing crime prevention schemes in a multi-agency setting: aspects of process in the Safer Cities programme.** Mike Sutton.1996. x + 53pp. (1 85893 691 8).

161. **Reducing criminality among young people: a sample of relevant programmes in the United Kingdom.** David Utting. 1996.vi + 112pp. (1 85893 744 2).

163. **Curfew orders with electronic monitoring.** George Mair and Ed Mortimer. 1996. x + 50pp. (1 85893 765 5).

Nos 159 and 162 are not published yet.

Research and Planning Unit Papers (RPUP)

81. **The welfare needs of unconvicted prisoners.** Diane Caddle and Sheila White. 1994.

82. **Racially motivated crime: a British Crime Survey analysis.** Natalie Aye Maung and Catriona Mirrlees-Black. 1994.

83. **Mathematical models for forecasting Passport demand.** Andy Jones and John MacLeod. 1994.

84. **The theft of firearms.** John Corkery. 1994.

85. **Equal opportunities and the Fire Service.** Tom Bucke. 1994.

86. **Drug Education Amongst Teenagers: a 1992 British Crime Survey Analysis.** Lizanne Dowds and Judith Redfern. 1995.

87. **Group 4 Prisoner Escort Service: a survey of customer satisfaction.** Claire Nee. 1994.

88. **Special Considerations: Issues for the Management and Organisation of the Volunteer Police.** Catriona Mirrlees-Black and Carole Byron. 1995.

89. **Self-reported drug misuse in England and Wales: findings from the 1992 British Crime Survey.** Joy Mott and Catriona Mirrlees-Black. 1995.

90. **Improving bail decisions: the bail process project, phase 1.** John Burrows, Paul Henderson and Patricia Morgan. 1995.

91. **Practitioners' views of the Criminal Justice Act: a survey of criminal justice agencies.** George Mair and Chris May. 1995.

92. **Obscene, threatening and other troublesome telephone calls to women in England and Wales: 1982-1992.** Wendy Buck, Michael Chatterton and Ken Pease. 1995.

93. **A survey of the prisoner escort and custody service provided by Group 4 and by Securicor Custodial Services.** Diane Caddle. 1995.

Research Findings

8. **Findings from the International Crime Survey.** Pat Mayhew. 1994.

9   **Fear of Crime: Findings from the 1992 British Crime Survey.** Catriona Mirrlees-Black and Natalie Aye Maung. 1994.

10. **Does the Criminal Justice system treat men and women differently?** Carol Hedderman and Mike Hough. 1994.

11. **Participation in Neighbourhood Watch: Findings from the 1992 British Crime Survey.** Lizanne Dowds and Pat Mayhew. 1994.

12. **Explaining Reconviction Rates: A Critical Analysis.** Charles Lloyd, George Mair and Mike Hough. 1995.

13. **Equal opportunities and the Fire Service.** Tom Bucke. 1994.

14. **Trends in Crime: Findings from the 1994 British Crime Survey.** Pat Mayhew, Catriona Mirrlees-Black and Natalie Aye Maung. 1994.

15. **Intensive Probation in England and Wales: an evaluation.** George Mair, Charles Lloyd, Claire Nee and Rae Sibbitt. 1995.

16. **The settlement of refugees in Britain.** Jenny Carey-Wood, Karen Duke, Valerie Karn and Tony Marshall. 1995.

17. **Young people, victimisation and the police: British Crime Survey findings on experiences and attitudes of 12- to 15- year-olds.** Natalie Aye Maung. 1995.

18. **Vietnamese Refugees since 1982.** Karen Duke and Tony Marshall. 1995.

19. **Supervision of Restricted Patients in the Community.** Suzanne Dell and Adrian Grounds. 1995.

20. **Videotaping children's evidence: an evaluation.** Graham Davies, Clare Wilson, Rebecca Mitchell and John Milsom. 1995.

21. **The mentally disordered and the police.** Graham Robertson, Richard Pearson and Robert Gibb. 1995.

22. **Preparing records of taped interviews.** Andrew Hooke and Jim Knox. 1995.

23. **Obscene, threatening and other troublesome telephone calls to women: Findings from the British Crime Survey.** Wendy Buck, Michael Chatterton and Ken Pease. 1995.

24. **Young people and crime.** John Graham and Ben Bowling. 1995.

25. **Anxiety about crime: Findings from the 1994 British Crime Survey.** Michael Hough. 1995.

26. **Crime against retail premises in 1993.** Catriona Mirrlees-Black and Alec Ross. 1995.

27. **Crime against manufacturing premises in 1993.** Catriona Mirrlees-Black and Alec Ross. 1995.

28. **Policing and the public: findings from the 1994 British Crime Survey.** Tom Bucke. 1995.

29. **The Child Witness Pack – An Evaluation.** Joyce Plotnikoff and Richard Woolfson. 1995.

30. **To scare straight or educate? The British experience of day visits to prison for young people.** Charles Lloyd. 1996.

31. **The ADT drug treatment programme at HMP Downview – a preliminary evaluation.** Elaine Player and Carol Martin. 1996.

32. **Wolds remand prison – an evaluation.** Keith Bottomley, Adrian James, Emma Clare and Alison Liebling. 1996.

33. **Drug misuse declared: results of the 1994 British Crime Survey.** Malcolm Ramsay and Andrew Percy. 1996.

34. **Crack cocaine and drugs-crime careers.** Howard Parker and Tim Bottomley. 1996.

35. **Imprisonment for fine default.** David Moxon and Claire Whittaker. 1996.

36. **Fine impositions and enforcement following the Criminal Justice Act 1993.** Elizabeth Charman, Bryan Gibson, Terry Honess and Rod Morgan. 1996.

37 **Victimisation in prisons.** Ian O'Donnell and Kimmett Edgar. 1996.

39 **Ethnic minorities, victimisation and racial harassment.** Marian Fitzgerald and Chris Hale. 1996

40 **Evaluating joint performance management between the police and the Crown Prosecution Service.** Andrew Hooke, Jim Knox and David Portas. 1996.

41 **Public attitudes to drug–related crime.** Sharon Grace. 1996.

42 **Domestic burglary schemes in the safer cities programme.** Paul Ekblom, Ho Law and Mike Sutton. 1996.

43   **Pakistani women's experience of domestic violence in Great Britain.** Salma Choudry. 1996.

44   **Witnesses with learning disabilities.** Andrew Sanders, Jane Creaton, Sophia Bird and Leanne Weber. 1996.

46   **Re–education programmes for violent men – an evaluation.** Russell Dobash, Rebecca Emerson Dobash, Kate Cavanagh and Ruth Lewis. 1996.

47   **Sentencing without a pre–sentence report.** Nigel Charles, Claire Whittaker and Caroline Ball. 1997

49   **Pace ten years on: a review of research.** David Brown. 1997.

Research Bulletin

The Research Bulletin is usually published twice each year and contains short articles on recent research.

Occasional Papers

Measurement of caseload weightings associated with the Children Act. Richard J. Gadsden and Graham J. Worsdale. 1994. (Available from the RSD Information and Publications Group).

Managing difficult prisoners: The Lincoln and Hull special units. Professor Keith Bottomley, Professor Norman Jepson, Mr Kenneth Elliott and Dr Jeremy Coid. 1994. (Available from the RSD Information and Publications Group).

The Nacro diversion initiative for mentally disturbed offenders: an account and an evaluation. Home Office, NACRO and Mental Health Foundation. 1994. (Available from the RSD Information and Publications Group).

Probation Motor Projects in England and Wales. J P Martin and Douglas Martin. 1994.

Community-based treatment of sex offenders: an evaluation of seven treatment programmes. R Beckett, A Beech, D Fisher and A S Fordham. 1994.

Videotaping children's evidence: an evaluation. Graham Davies, Clare Wilson, Rebecca Mitchell and John Milsom. 1995.

Managing the needs of female prisoners. Allison Morris, Chris Wilkinson, Andrea Tisi, Jane Woodrow and Ann Rockley. 1995.

Local information points for volunteers. Michael Locke, Nick Richards, Lorraine Down, Jon Griffiths and Roger Worgan. 1995.

Mental disorder in remand prisoners. Anthony Maden, Caecilia J. A. Taylor, Deborah Brooke and John Gunn. 1996.

An evaluation of prison work and training. Frances Simon and Claire Corbett. 1996.

The Impact of the National Lottery on the Horse-Race Betting Levy. Simon Field. 1996.

Requests for Publications

Home Office Research Studies from 143 onwards, *Research and Planning Unit Papers, Research Findings and Research Bulletins* are available **subject to availability** on request from:

Research and Statistics Directorate
Information and Publications Group
Room 1308, Home Office
Apollo House
36 Wellesley Road
Croydon CR9 3RR
Telephone: 0181 760 8340
Fascimile: 0181 760 8364
Internet: http//www.open.gov.uk/home_off/rsdhome.htp
E-mail: rsd.ha apollo @ gtnet.gov.u.

Occasional Papers can be purchased from:
Home Office
Publications Unit
50 Queen Anne's Gate
London SW1H 9AT
Telephone: 0171 273 2302

Home Office Research Studies prior to 143 can be purchased from:

HMSO Publications Centre

(Mail, fax and telephone orders only)
PO Box 276, London SW8 5DT
Telephone orders: 0171-873 9090
General enquiries: 0171-873 0011
(queuing system in operation for both numbers)
Fax orders: 0171-873 8200

*And also from **HMSO Bookshops***